This book may be returned to any Wiltshire
library. To renew this book phone your library
or visit the website: www.wiltshire.gov.uk

Wiltshire
COUNTY COUNCIL

CHILDREN, EDUCATION & LIBRARIES   LM6.108.5

GEOGRAPHY FACT FILES

RIVERS

Mandy Ross

HODDER
Wayland

an imprint of Hodder Children's Books

GEOGRAPHY FACT FILES

Produced by Monkey Puzzle Media Ltd

Gissing's Farm, Fressingfield, Suffolk IP21 5SH, UK

First published in 2004 by Hodder Wayland

An imprint of Hodder Children's Books

Text copyright © 2004 Hodder Wayland

Volume copyright © 2004 Hodder Wayland

Editor	Catherine Burch
Designer	Jamie Asher
Picture Researcher	Lynda Lines and Frances Bailey
Illustrator	Michael Posen
Consultant	Michael Allaby

Printed in China

Cover picture: Colorado River, USA

Title page picture: A meandering river in Alaska, USA..

British Library Cataloguing in Publication Data

Ross, Mandy

 Rivers. – (Geography fact files)

 1.Rivers – Juvenile literature 2.Stream ecology – Juvenile literature

 I.Title

 551.4'83

 ISBN 07502 4403 8

Acknowledgements

We are grateful to the following for permission to reproduce photographs: Aerofilms.com 17 bottom; Associated Press 11 bottom (Apichart Weera Wong); Corbis *back cover bottom* (Ales Fevzer), 13 bottom (Hulton-Deutsch), 27 (Kevin Fleming), 42 (Ales Fevzer); Digital Vision 47; Ecoscene 41 (Stephen Coyne); FLPA 6 (Minden Pictures), 29 bottom (David Hosking), 37 top (Skylight); Getty images *front cover* (Jeremy Woodhouse); Nature Picture Library 10 (Pete Oxford), 19 (Paul N Johnson), 21 top (A and S Chandola), 23 top (Vincent Munier), 24 (John Cancalosi), 28 (Staffan Widstrand), 40 top (Jean Roche); NHPA 4 (David Woodfall), 18 (NASA/ T&T Stack), 20 (David Woodfall), 40 bottom (David Woodfall); Edward Parker 25; Popperfoto 38, 39 (Juda Ngwenya/Reuters); Robert Harding Picture Library 3 middle (T Waltham), 3 bottom (Paul Allen), 5 bottom (Roy Rainford), 9, 11 top, 14, 15 (T Waltham), 22 (Paul Allen), 23 bottom (Gary Schultz), 29 top (Gavin Hellier); Science Photo Library 36 (Martin Bond); Still Pictures 1 (S J Krasemann), 3 top (BAV/Helga Lade GmbH), 5 top (BAV/Helga Lade GmbH), 17 top (S J Krasemann), 26 (Hartmut Schwarzbach), 33 bottom (Jorgen Schytte), 35 (Jim Wark), 37 bottom (Michael Coupard), 43 (J Sackermann/Das Fotoarchiv), 44 (Uniphoto International); Topham Picturepoint 13 top (Rob Crandall/Image Works), 21 bottom (Tom Brakefield/ Image Works), 30 (Jim Pickerell/Image Works), 31 (Lee Snider/Image Works), 32 (Owen Humphreys/PA), 46 (Lee Snider/Image Works); WaterAid 45 (Jon Spaull).

Hodder Childen's Books

A division of Hodder Headline Limited

338 Euston Road, London NW1 3BH

CONTENTS

The words that are explained in the glossary
are printed in **bold** the first time they are
mentioned in the text.

WHAT IS A RIVER?

A river is a large stream of fresh flowing water. High in the mountains, small streams gather together to form a river rushing down through hills and valleys. Lower down most rivers flow more slowly through flatter land until they reach the sea. River environments are very important because all life needs water to survive.

Most streams begin high in the mountains, like this one in Snowdonia, Wales.

There are rivers all around the world. Rivers flow through icy landscapes, freezing over during the coldest seasons. They flow through tropical rain forests and through deserts. Many cities are built on the banks of great rivers, growing out of villages inhabited since ancient times.

Rivers are a source of life for humans, animals and plants. They offer fish to eat, water to drink and to irrigate crops, they provide transport routes and are popular places for recreation. The power of flowing water can be harnessed to create **renewable energy**. However, water can also be dangerous. When rivers flood, or when the water is polluted, rivers can threaten the very life that they sustain.

FACT FILE

RIVER FACTS
• The world's longest river is the River Nile in Africa. It is about 6,650 km long.
• The Roe River in Montana, USA, is one of the world's shortest rivers. It is just 61 m long – about as long as 15 cars!
• Rivers make up only a tiny fraction of the world's fresh water – just 0.003 per cent. Lakes and inland seas make up 0.6 per cent and the rest is in ice caps and **glaciers**, **groundwater** and in the soil.

THE MISSISSIPPI RIVER, USA

The name Mississippi comes from Algonkian, a Native American language, from the words *misi*, meaning 'big', and *sipi*, meaning 'water'. The Mississippi River (left) starts as a clear winding stream. Many rivers join it along its 5,971 km course, including the Missouri, Ohio and Red Rock. Downriver, it stretches over 2 km wide in places. The Mississippi loops and curves along its floodplain, but has been straightened in places to allow ships to pass more safely. It is one of the busiest shipping waterways in the world.

The Mississippi passes through 10 US states and is the longest river in North America.

Below Many great cities have grown up at a crossing point over a river, like the Seine in Paris, France.

River water is a shared and precious resource. What is done to a river in one place may affect it a long way downstream, so rivers must be treated carefully to protect our own needs and for the wildlife that depends on them.

RIVERS AND THE WATER CYCLE

Rivers are part of a never-ending **water cycle**. Most rivers start high in the mountains where plenty of rain and snow fall. Rainwater and melted snow flow down the mountains and hills, and eventually out into the salty ocean. There the sun and wind cause some of the water to evaporate, then **condense** into tiny droplets forming clouds, and later fall as rain. So the whole cycle starts again.

GREAT RIVERS

S ome of the great rivers of the world flow thousands of kilometres, travelling across whole continents. Some are so wide that if you stand on one bank the other bank is too far away to be seen. These great rivers can be seen better from the air or even from space. Which is the world's greatest river? It depends what you measure.

There are many different ways to measure the size of a river. One way is to measure its length, from its beginning, or **source**, to the place where it meets the sea, called the mouth. Rivers do not flow in straight lines, but flow round bends and curves, so the measurement has to follow all the curves.

Another way of comparing the size of rivers is to measure the amount of water flowing in them, called the **discharge**. The discharge changes during the year, so an average figure is usually given.

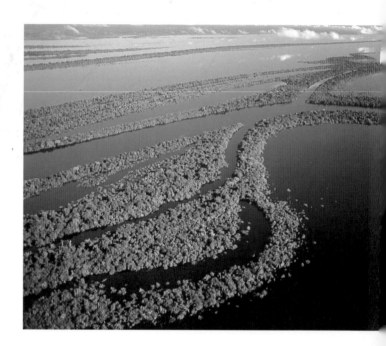

For most of its length the River Amazon is between 6 and 10 km wide.

FACT FILE

THE WORLD'S LONGEST RIVERS

RIVER	OUTFLOW	LENGTH (km) including main tributaries
Nile	Mediterranean Sea	6,650
Amazon-Ucayali-Apurimac	South Atlantic Ocean	6,400
Yangtze	East China Sea	6,300
Mississippi-Missouri-Red Rock	Gulf of Mexico	5,971
Yenisey-Baikal-Selenga	Kara Sea	5,540
Yellow River	East China Sea	5,464
Ob-Irtysh	Gulf of Ob	5,410
Parana	South Atlantic Ocean	4,880
Congo	Atlantic Ocean	4,700
Amur-Argun	Sea of Okhotsk	4,444

RIVERS WITH THE LARGEST DRAINAGE AREA

RIVER	LOCATION	DRAINAGE AREA (000 km²)
Amazon	South America	7,180
Congo	Africa	3,822
Mississippi-Missouri	North America	3,221
Ob	Siberia	2,975
Nile	Africa	2,881
Parana	S. America	2,650
Yenisey–Angara	Siberia	2,605
Lena	Asia	2,490
Niger	Africa	2,092
Yangtze	China	1,970

A third way of comparing rivers is to measure the area of land that drains into the river. This measurement includes all the land that is drained by streams and small rivers or **tributaries** that flow into the main river. This total area is called a river's **drainage area** or basin.

The Amazon is only the second-longest river in the world, but it has by far the biggest discharge. This is because the Amazon has the biggest drainage area, including about 40 per cent of the continent of South America. Most of the rivers of the northern half of South America flow into the Amazon, because mountains and high land cut off other routes to the sea. Much of the continent's water flows east into the Amazon, creating a giant river. About one-fifth of all the world's river water flows out of the Amazon into the Atlantic Ocean!

A map showing the world's greatest rivers.

SPRINGS AND SOURCES

Where do rivers start? Most begin on high ground or in the mountains. Many of the world's greatest rivers start as **springs** and tiny streams in high mountains. For instance the source of the River Ganges in Asia is high in the Himalayan mountains. Searching for the source of the river is a challenge that has inspired many explorers.

High in the mountains there is heavy rain and snowfall. The rain that falls on the mountainsides runs quickly down the steep slopes into little channels called rills. These rills join together to form small streams, and as the streams run down the mountain they also join together, gradually forming a wide river.

Streams and rivers are also fed by melt-water, which flows down the mountainsides when warmer weather causes snow and ice high in the mountains to melt. If the weather warms up quickly, melting a lot of snow, rivers can suddenly get much deeper, and sometimes flood.

The making of a river.

PEOPLE FILE

WHO FOUND THE NILE SOURCE?

Over two thousand years ago the Greek historian Herodotus wrote: 'Of the source of the Nile no one can give any account.' In fact, the River Nile has two sources, the Blue Nile and the White Nile. The first European to see the source of the Blue Nile was Father Pedro Páez, a Spanish Jesuit, in 1618. In 1937 a German explorer, Dr Burkhart Waldecker, traced the source of the White Nile back to its southernmost source, in Burundi. A small pyramid there now marks Waldecker's discovery with the words: 'Caput Nili – Source of the Nile'.

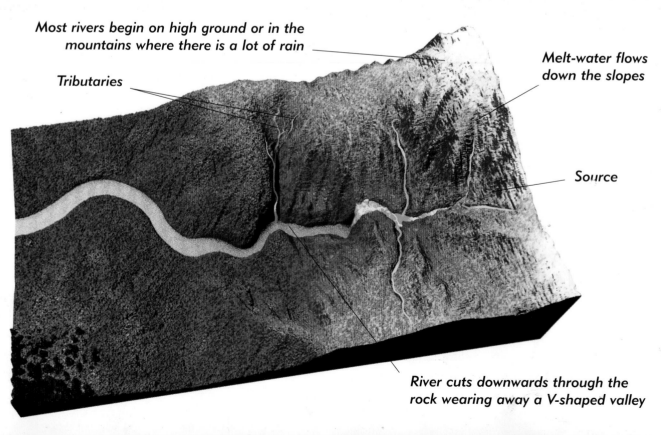

Most rivers begin on high ground or in the mountains where there is a lot of rain

Tributaries

Melt-water flows down the slopes

Source

River cuts downwards through the rock wearing away a V-shaped valley

Other rivers start from a source bubbling out of the rocks, called a spring. Some kinds of rock are **porous** – that is, water can sink into the rock. In areas of porous rock, such as sandstone or limestone, rainwater trickles through the rock and then flows underground until it emerges from the earth, forming a spring.

On low-lying ground and in depressions water may gather in hollows, or on the surface of the land, causing the ground to be **saturated**. This is known as a bog, marsh or swamp. Water trickles out of bogs into streams and rivers.

LOCATION FILE

THE RHINE AND RHÔNE

Two of Europe's great rivers, the Rhine (above) and the Rhône, flow from sources close together high in the Swiss Alps but they flow out in opposite directions. The Rhine flows 1,390 km north and west and out through the Netherlands into the North Sea. It is an important shipping route. The 813 km-long Rhône flows south through France and out into the Mediterranean Sea. Its route passes through mountains, making it difficult for large ships to navigate.

Above **Barges on the River Rhine. Since Roman times, the Rhine has been vitally important for travel and trade.**

DOWN THE MOUNTAIN

As rivers flow they loosen rocks and soil, especially when they flood. They may carry along great boulders and huge quantities of mud, transporting them to another place along the river's bed or sometimes carrying them all the way to the sea. The rocks are smashed and crushed into smaller pieces, then they are ground into tiny grains of sand called **sediment**. Soil is washed into the river by rainfall and during flooding adds to the river's sediment. Each of a river's tributaries brings sediment from the land it drains.

SEDIMENT

As long as the river is flowing quickly, sediment is carried along in the water. Where the water starts to flow more slowly the sediment may fall to the bottom of the river's bed. This clogs up the river and makes it dangerous for larger boats travelling along its course. The sediment needs to be dug or **dredged** out of the river's bed to make it safe for boats again.

Some sediment is carried all the way to the river's mouth and into the sea. In Asia, the Ganges, Yellow River and Brahmaputra carry one-fifth of the world's sediment into the sea.

The tributaries of the River Amazon are each a different colour, because they bring sediment made up from the different kinds of soil and rock they flow over.

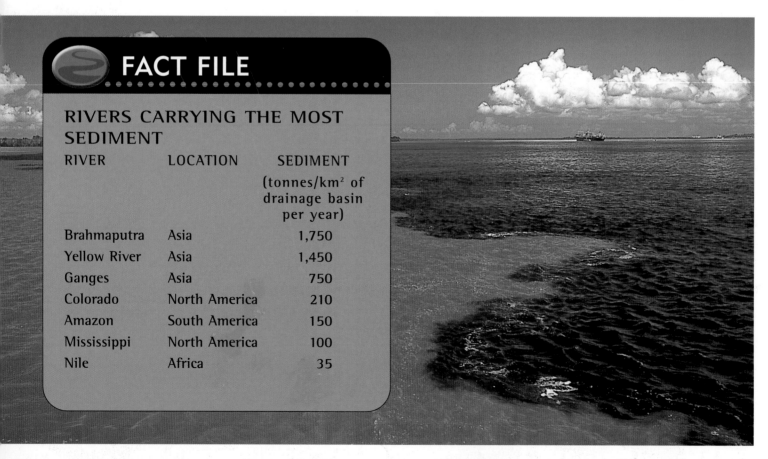

FACT FILE

RIVERS CARRYING THE MOST SEDIMENT

RIVER	LOCATION	SEDIMENT (tonnes/km² of drainage basin per year)
Brahmaputra	Asia	1,750
Yellow River	Asia	1,450
Ganges	Asia	750
Colorado	North America	210
Amazon	South America	150
Mississippi	North America	100
Nile	Africa	35

FORESTS – OR FLOODS?

Tree roots help to hold the land together so that less soil is **eroded** away as water runs across it. Trees and plants absorb rainwater in the soil, which also helps to prevent flooding. Where forests have been cut down, especially on steep hillsides, soil is more easily eroded and this can lead to serious flooding and dangerous landslips.

Above **Deforestation in South Africa. Forest may be cut down, especially in poorer countries, for timber and to clear land for farming or construction.**

 LOCATION FILE

NORTHERN THAILAND

In December 2001 in the Phetchabun region of northern Thailand, more than 70 people were killed in **flash floods**. Relief work was hampered by mud and tree trunks that were swept down the mountainsides. Flash floods were always a problem in the region, but they have become more frequent and much more dangerous since huge areas of forest were cut down locally.

Villagers search through a house badly damaged by a flash flood in the Phetchabun province of Thailand.

VALLEYS AND WATERFALLS

River valleys are formed in a constant process. As a river flows down over mountains and hills it cuts down into the rock. Over hundreds of thousands of years the flowing water can cut deep valleys and dramatic waterfalls, changing the landscape.

VALLEYS

Stones and gravel grind the river's bed, gouging out a narrow V-shaped channel. In areas of softer rock, such as sandstone, rivers can erode the rock more quickly and dramatically than in areas of hard rock, such as granite.

During the ice ages, glaciers cut great valleys as they flowed out towards the sea. Unlike rivers, glaciers form a wide U-shape valley. Active glaciers are still at work in cold regions around the world. The longest glacier in the world is in the Antarctic, it is 515 km long.

Some river valleys, called **wadis**, run through deserts. They are usually dry because so little rain falls in the desert. Wadis were formed thousands of years ago when the Earth's climate was different from how it is today. Wadis were cut when there was enough rain to let rivers flow, but today wadis are only ever filled if exceptional rainfall causes a flash flood.

The action of a river carves a V-shaped valley.

The action of a glacier carves a U-shaped valley.

WATERFALLS

• The world's highest waterfall – the Angel Falls (right) on the River Churun in Venezuela, South America – has a total drop of 979 m.
• The widest waterfall is the Khon Cataracts in Laos, Asia. It is not very deep, but over 12 km wide!
• The waterfall with the most water flowing per second is the Boyoma Falls in the Democratic Republic of Congo, Africa. There the water flows at a rate of 17,000 m³ per second.

Angel Falls in Venezuela, the world's highest falls.

WATERFALLS AND RAPIDS

A waterfall is a place where a river drops vertically to a lower level. Many waterfalls are formed when a river flows over different kinds of rock. The water wears away soft rock more quickly than hard rock, so the hard rock remains while, over hundreds of thousands of years, the soft rock is eroded. This creates a cliff edge over which the water flows. Some spectacular waterfalls, called hanging valleys, are created by glaciers.

Rapids are places where the river drops quickly, but not as steeply as at a waterfall. Rapids form where the rock is too hard for the river to wear down a more even slope.

BLONDIN

In 1859, the French acrobat Jean-Francois Gravelet (1824-1897), known as Blondin, crossed the Niagara gorge, just by the Falls, by tightrope between the USA and Canada. The tightrope was 335 m long, suspended 49 m above the water. He repeated the feat many times, backwards, blindfolded, and once sitting down midway to cook and eat an omelette!

Blondin, the French acrobat, performs a tightrope walk high above the Niagara River.

GORGES, CANYONS, CAVES

Canyons and gorges are very steep valleys, or gashes, in the landscape where a river has cut deep into the rock. Many caves are formed by rivers, too, where the water is flowing underground. Gorges, **canyons** and caves all show the natural power of a river, eroding rock over millions of years.

Canyons can range in size from narrow slits in hard rock to enormous trenches. A river flows at the bottom, constantly carving away at the rock beneath.

The Grand Canyon in the USA is the world's deepest, longest and widest canyon. It was carved out by the Colorado River. Down its sides, the Grand Canyon reveals layers of different coloured rock. These layers show the history of the Earth's rocks. The oldest rocks are at the bottom. Some, called granite and schist, are up to 4 billion years old – among the oldest rocks on the Earth.

 FACT FILE

DEEP DOWN
• The Grand Canyon (right) is 443 km long and its steep walls are up to 1,737 m deep. At its widest point, the canyon is 29 km wide.
• The deepest river in the world is China's Yangtze River, where it passes through the 600 m-high Three Gorges. Here the river flows up to 180 m deep. A new **dam** on the Yangtze River means that the rising water will eventually cover these gorges.

The rocks at the bottom of the Grand Canyon date from between 2 and 4 billion years ago while those in the top layer are about 250 million years old. Rocks younger than 250 million years have been eroded away.

An underground river wore away this large passage, called Clearwater Cave, in Mulu National Park, Sarawak, Malaysia. The cave is 107 km long.

CAVES AND POTHOLES

Caves and potholes are created by underground rivers wearing away at the rock. Most caves are in areas where there are thick layers of limestone rock. Limestone is porous rock, so water can seep through it. The water flows underground along cracks between layers of rock. As more and more water flows through the cracks, they grow wider. The flowing water forms an underground river which is able to erode a cave out of the limestone. Underground rivers usually come to the surface through a spring or cave entrance.

Exploring caves, or potholing, is a popular hobby. Potholers squeeze through narrow cracks to try to find new caves. They use underwater equipment to swim along underground rivers. Potholing can be dangerous, especially if there is sudden heavy rain which makes the underground river level rise.

 LOCATION FILE

WORLD'S LONGEST CAVE

The Mammoth Cave National Park and Flint Ridge Cave System in Kentucky, USA, together make up a 500 km-long network of underground caves, rivers, and lakes. Over 50 types of cave creatures have been discovered there, including blind fish and colourless spiders, specially adapted to life in this dark, watery environment.

MEANDERS AND LAKES

1n the mountains, river water travels fast down steep slopes, but once a river reaches lower land it flows more slowly. The river cuts a course through the softest bits of ground on its way to sea, flowing in loops and curves, carving out a wide valley bottom. Lakes may be formed where a river flows into a lower area of land.

MEANDERS

The loops and curves of a slow-moving river are called **meanders**. The water flows fastest around the outer edge of the meander, and over time this erodes the outer edge, gradually widening the valley. On the inner bank of each meander the water flows more slowly, depositing sediment there. This causes the entire meander system to advance slowly downstream.

Sometimes when the river is in high flow or flood, it cuts across the neck of a meander to create a straighter path. This can leave a crescent-shaped lake called an oxbow lake. Oxbow lakes do not last very long, because they are no longer being filled by the river's flow. Over time they fill up with sediment and plants grow, forming bogs and swamps.

FACT FILE

WORLD'S LARGEST LAKES, 2001

LAKE	LOCATION	AREA (km²)
Caspian Sea	Asia	386,400
Lake Superior	North America	82,100
Lake Victoria	Africa	69,485
Lake Huron	North America	59,600
Lake Michigan	North America	57,800
Aral Sea	Asia	33,800
Lake Tanganyika	Africa	32,900
Lake Baikal	Siberia	31,500
Great Bear Lake	Canada	31,153
Lake Nyasa	Africa	29,604

This diagram shows how a river meanders.

Sediment is deposited on the inner edge of the meander

The river flows fastest around the outer edge of the meander

Sometimes the river cuts off the neck of the meander. With no current flowing in or out of the meander, sediment is deposited and the entrance and exit become blocked, forming an oxbow lake.

The amazing contortions of a meandering river in Alaska, USA. You can see an oxbow lake in the centre of the picture.

LAKES

Lakes are formed where a river flows through a hollow in the ground, or where the river is blocked. Water gathers and fills up the hollow. A stream or river flows out of the lowest edge of the lake. Some lakes, however, have no outflow, and only lose water by evaporation. In some cases, such as Australia's Lake Eyre, these lakes can become very salty as the minerals in the water become more concentrated. Some lakes are so large they are called seas, even though they are enclosed by land.

 LOCATION FILE

SHREWSBURY

The historic town of Shrewsbury (right), in the border country between England and Wales, is built on land contained within a loop of the River Severn. The river forms a natural defence around the walled town, which made it a safe stronghold during times of war in the Middle Ages.

This aerial view of Shrewsbury shows how the old town was built inside a loop of the river.

THE RIVER'S MOUTH

A river ends where it pours out its water into another river, into the sea or, in some places, into a lake. This place is called the river's mouth. Here the river brings its water, as well as all the mud and pollution it may have collected on the way.

Almost all river water flows out into the sea or the ocean, with a few exceptions. The River Volga in Russia, for example, actually flows inland into the world's largest lake, the Caspian Sea. Many rivers flow into the sea with such force that they continue to flow for several kilometres after reaching the sea. The Amazon pours four times more water into the sea than the next biggest river, the Congo in Africa. Water from the Amazon flows out into the salty sea water for 160 km. The river water floats above the sea water, because fresh water is less dense than salt water.

A view of the Yangtze River delta from space shows how the river empties into the sea.

FACT FILE

RIVERS WITH MOST WATER DISCHARGED AT RIVER MOUTH

RIVER	LOCATION	WATER DISCHARGE (m^3 of water per second)
Amazon	South America	180,000
Congo	Africa	42,000
Yangtze	China	35,000
Orinoco	South America	28,000
Brahmaputra	Asia	20,000
Yenisey-Angara	Siberia	19,600
Parana	South America	19,500
Mississippi	North America	17,545
Lena	Asia	16,400
Mekong	Asia	15,900

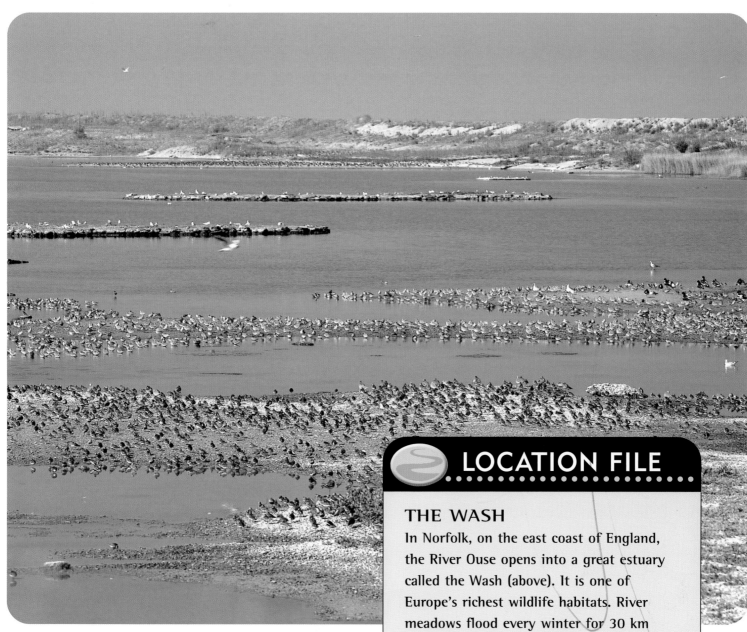

LOCATION FILE

THE WASH

In Norfolk, on the east coast of England, the River Ouse opens into a great estuary called the Wash (above). It is one of Europe's richest wildlife habitats. River meadows flood every winter for 30 km along the river's banks. There are also mudflats, salt-marsh and flooded gravel pits. Huge flocks of ducks, geese and other birds migrate here from the Arctic north to spend the winter. In the summer, wading birds such as lapwings breed in the estuary.

Above **Flocks of birds on a river estuary in Norfolk, UK.**

ESTUARIES

Most rivers grow wider as they flow into the sea. This wider area at the river's mouth is called an **estuary**. Here the river water meets the tidal water from the sea. When the tide is coming in, sea water flows back up into the estuary for some distance.

As the river opens out into the estuary the water flows more slowly. The mud and sediment in its water drops to the bottom of the river's bed and along its banks. When the tide goes out, this river mud is left uncovered. These areas are called **mudflats**. At low tide mudflats are an important wildlife habitat, offering rich feeding grounds for wading birds such as sandpipers, who dig with their beaks for burrowing creatures beneath the surface of the mud.

DELTAS AND SWAMPS

Deltas – the wide open mouths of many rivers – are so-called because they form a sort of delta shape. Delta, or Δ, is the fourth letter in the Greek alphabet, equivalent to our 'D'. Its shape is how the Nile Delta looked to the ancient Greeks living to the north. The word delta is now used to describe a place where a river flows in many separate channels out into the sea. The Ganges, Amazon, Mississippi and the Nile all form a delta where they meet the sea.

DELTA SHAPES

Deltas can form different shapes. Some deltas form the shape of an arc; others look like the outstretched fingers of a hand, or like a bird's foot. These deltas are called bird's foot deltas. Some deltas are very wide indeed, stretching for tens or even hundreds of kilometres.

Deltas are formed where a river slows down as it reaches the sea. Because it is flowing more slowly, the sediment and mud it has been carrying drops on to the river's bed and its banks. As the delta builds up, the river creates small streams, or creeks, through which the water flows to the sea. These are called distributaries.

FACT FILE

DELTA SIZES

• The biggest delta in the world is formed by two great rivers, the Ganges and the Brahmaputra, in Bangladesh. Their joint delta covers an area of about 60,000 km².

• Swamps on the Mississippi Delta (right) are shrinking by up to 100 km² a year, partly because dams are reducing the amount of sediment carried by the river, and because of reduced soil erosion from farming.

Salt-marshes and low islands in the great Mississippi Delta.

LOW-LYING ISLANDS

Over many hundreds and thousands of years, layers of sediment build up. Grasses, reeds and other marshy plants which can live in salty tide-water start to take root in the mud banks. Their roots stop the mud from being washed away. Very gradually, as the vegetation dies back and grows again, the mud changes into soil, and low, flat islands are formed in the river.

Low-lying land formed in a delta is often flooded when the river-level is high, or when storms and cyclones send huge waves crashing in from the sea. However, delta land is very fertile and it attracts people to live and farm there, even though there is great danger from flooding. In 1990, 140,000 people were killed by floods caused by a cyclone in the Ganges Delta.

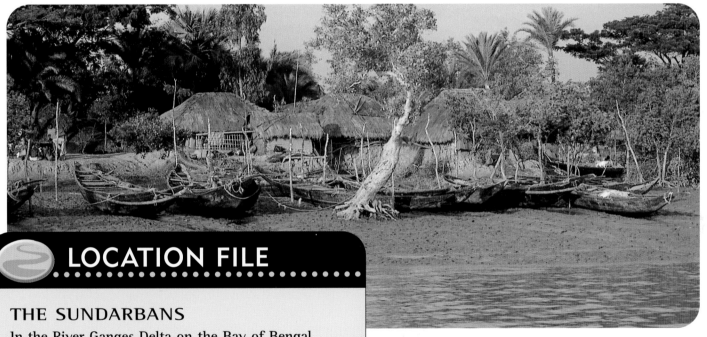

● LOCATION FILE

THE SUNDARBANS

In the River Ganges Delta on the Bay of Bengal, there are over 50 low islands, called the Sundarbans (above). The Sundarbans contains the largest area of mangrove trees in the world. Mangrove trees are like trees growing on stilts, to survive on land covered by sea at high tide. Many rare creatures live in this unique habitat, including Bengal tigers (right), crocodiles and golden eagles.

Above **A fishing village in the Sundarbans, West Bengal, India.**

Right **Rare Bengal tigers live in the mangrove swamps in the Sundarbans.**

RIVER WILDLIFE

A river is a rich and complex wildlife habitat. Rivers and river banks are the natural home for many kinds of fish, birds, insects and other animals. Fish feed on smaller creatures as well as weeds, reeds and algae. In turn, the fish provide a nourishing food source for birds, reptiles and mammals – including humans.

VARIETY OF LIFE

Tropical rivers support an astounding range of wildlife. As well as fish, the River Plata in South America has caimans (a type of crocodile), many types of water snake, frogs, toads and freshwater crabs. Large birds such as herons, cormorants and storks come to catch fish. Even in the coldest environments, rivers provide a habitat for a wide range of wildlife. The icy River Ob in Siberia, for instance, has over 50 species of fish.

In Africa, land animals come to the river bank to drink. Elephants need to drink 135–225 litres of water per day. Animals coming to drink may also feed on plants growing there, catch fish from the river and prey on other animals that come to drink there.

Rivers provide vital drinking water for many animals, such as these lions.

BEAVERS

Beavers are large rodents. They live beside rivers and lakes, mostly in North America. Beavers build dams to make small lakes where they are safe from predators. They build dams with twigs, branches and logs, with layers of gravel or mud. Beaver dams can divert or block the flow of rivers and streams.

A beaver gnawing at a tree.

FOOD CHAINS

In the wild, animals survive by eating either plants or other animals. Living things are linked as if in a chain, each one being the food for the next one in the series. Plants are always at the bottom of the chain, with large, hunting animals at the top. For instance, pondweed is eaten by ducks, which are eaten by foxes. This pattern is called a food chain.

If one part of the food chain is harmed, other creatures in the chain will also be affected. If fish are poisoned by pollution, animals which eat the fish may be poisoned too. If all the fish die, other animals may die because they have no food.

SALMON MIGRATION

• Salmon breed in rivers. The young salmon then swim out to sea, but return as adults to breed, often travelling thousands of miles to swim back up the very river where they hatched.
• Salmon can tell the particular river by its smell.
• Some types of salmon die soon after breeding. Others survive to make the journey again.

A grizzly bear catches a salmon as it leaps up a waterfall.

HARVESTING THE RIVER

Since ancient times humans have harvested rivers for fish and for plants, such as reeds. Ice was harvested from rivers, too, before the invention of refrigerators. Today, large-scale commercial production of fish is increasing.

All around the world, people living beside rivers **exploit** their produce. Fish, shellfish and waterfowl provide a rich source of protein. On the River Yenisey in Siberia, local people catch fish such as carp and perch, as well as sturgeon whose eggs are prized as the luxury food caviar.

Food crops such as watercress and samphire provide vitamins and minerals. River plants such as reeds can be used for weaving or building roofs. Just as on land, river farmers encourage and develop crops that grow naturally in the river environment.

FISH FARMING

Wild fish stocks in the rivers and oceans are under threat as the fishing industry grows larger and more efficient. In many parts of the world overfishing has caused a huge drop in the number of fish. There are not enough fish left in the wild to breed and replace those that are caught. In response, fish farming is on the increase around the world.

Fishermen set their nets at the edge of the River Yenisey in Siberia, Russia. The Yenisey has abundant fish of more than 30 different species.

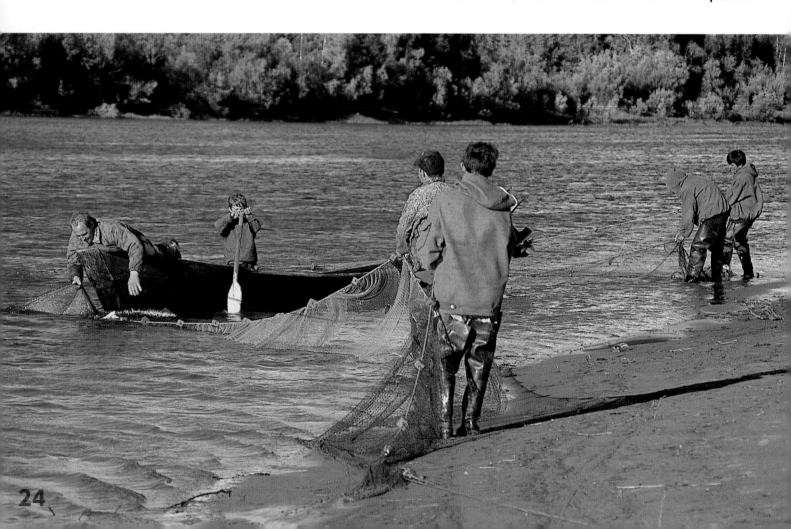

Fish farms breed and grow fish to sell for food. This provides a steady supply of fish, without reducing the number of wild fish even further. Reduced fishing in the wild allows fish populations time to grow again.

PERU, SOUTH AMERICA

Local people in Pucullpa, a poor area of Peru, are experimenting with fish farms in ponds dug beside the Amazon. Small, family-run fish farms are cheap and sustainable. Pig or chicken waste is dropped in the water, encouraging the growth of water plants which the fish feed on. The fish farmers can either eat the fish or sell them to raise money for their families.

FACT FILE

WORLD FISH FARMING FIGURES

(PUBLISHED IN 2002)

• Fish from fish farms (including those in seas and lakes) made up 15% of animal protein eaten around the world.

• An estimated 35 million people worked in fishing and fish-farming.

• Fish-farm production was worth a total of over US$50 billion (£30 billion).

• More than 210 different types of fish and plants were produced in fish farms.

China has a long history of fish farming. Typically, baby fish (fry) are allowed to grow in ponds next to the river and are then released into the river

There are fish farms in seas, lakes, **reservoirs** and rivers; some are huge, commercial concerns, others are small, family businesses. Many types of fish and shellfish are grown and harvested in river fish farms. There are even alligator farms in rivers in hot and tropical areas.

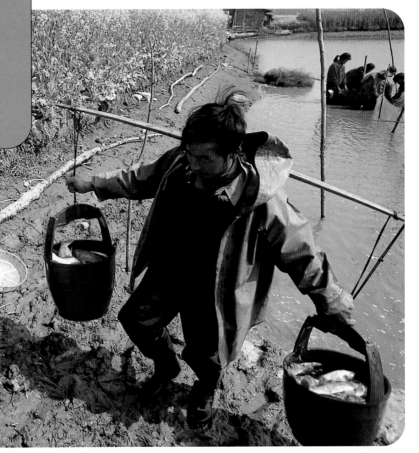

PROTECTING RIVERS

Rivers are vital for the wildlife in the water and on the banks, and they are also important for humans, but they are fragile environments. Rivers are natural drains, which can become polluted when they are used to drain away chemical or industrial waste. Building on or near riverbanks reduces the habitat available for wildlife.

Most people's drinking water comes from rivers and reservoirs. In developed countries, water is purified, or cleaned, before it is delivered to people's homes. Unfortunately in many of the world's poorest countries people have no choice but to use rivers for drinking, washing, and sometimes for carrying away untreated sewage. Millions of people around the world have no clean drinking water. Drinking dirty water can bring poor health and dangerous diseases.

A woman in Nepal has to wash her pots in a polluted river.

FACT FILE

POLLUTION ACCIDENTS

• In January 2000, huge amounts of cyanide-laden water spilled out of an abandoned mine in Romania into the rivers Szamos and Tisza. All living creatures were killed in a 400-km stretch of the river. Fortunately the rivers have now recovered.

• Thousands of fish and birds were killed in the Guadiamar River in Spain in 1998 when poisonous sludge spilled into a river after a mine reservoir broke its banks.

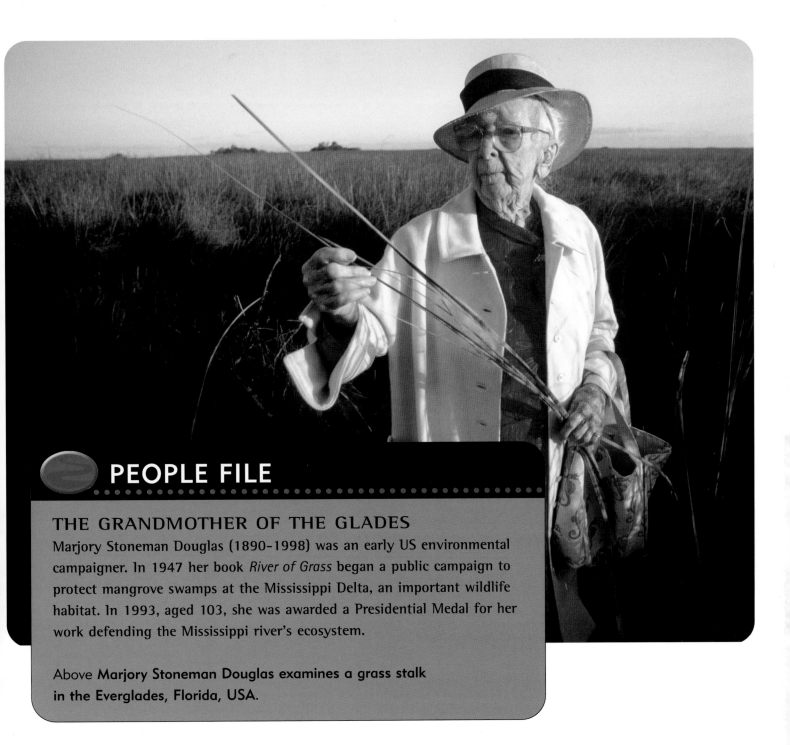

THE GRANDMOTHER OF THE GLADES

Marjory Stoneman Douglas (1890-1998) was an early US environmental campaigner. In 1947 her book *River of Grass* began a public campaign to protect mangrove swamps at the Mississippi Delta, an important wildlife habitat. In 1993, aged 103, she was awarded a Presidential Medal for her work defending the Mississippi river's ecosystem.

Above **Marjory Stoneman Douglas examines a grass stalk in the Everglades, Florida, USA.**

POLLUTION

Rivers and streams can become polluted in many ways, such as when waste from factories is poured into them, or when pesticides used in farming run off the soil and into streams and rivers, harming the wildlife in and around them. Another threat is from old coal, lead and tin mines. When old mines are closed the mining tunnels and shafts fill up with water, and the water becomes polluted by the metal and rusty machinery. The dirty water flows away, eventually joining a stream or river.

CAMPAIGNING TO PROTECT THE ENVIRONMENT

Many countries have passed laws to try to keep rivers clean and to protect the environment. Farmers and companies who pollute rivers with chemicals, or by dumping waste, must pay large fines. Environmental groups campaign for stronger protection for rivers and wildlife, and to provide clean drinking water for everyone on the planet. As a result of this, river water is improving now throughout the industrialized world, after centuries of increasing pollution.

RIVER CIVILIZATIONS

The earliest human civilizations were built near rivers in Egypt, India and China. Rivers provided a natural water supply and people could travel and transport goods down a river more easily than across land before roads were built.

FIRST CITIES

The world's first cities grew up around five thousand years ago in Mesopotamia (modern Turkey, Iraq and Syria). The name Mesopotamia in Greek means 'the land between two rivers'. These two rivers, the Tigris and the Euphrates, flooded their banks every spring. The regular flooding laid down a rich layer of fertilizing mud which made the surrounding plains rich and fertile for planting crops. The human population flourished with plentiful food supplies, and cities grew up.

The civilization of ancient Egypt also depended on the flooding of a river, the Nile. The Nile valley is a long, narrow fertile strip of land surrounded by hot, dry desert. Boats linked the north and south of the country, travelling along the Nile downstream on the current, and upstream using sails.

EARLY FARMING

The farmers of Mesopotamia and ancient Egypt built complex **irrigation** systems to bring water to their crops. **Canals**, ditches and reservoirs controlled and channelled the annual floods. Irrigation allowed crops to be grown, including wheat, pulses, vegetables and fruit. Flax (a type of plant) was woven to make linen for clothing, sails and ropes. In Egypt, papyrus was grown to produce a type of paper. Thus rivers enabled early human technologies and the development of agriculture.

A worker with a modern irrigation pump bringing water from the River Nile to farmland in Egypt. River water is still vital for agriculture, just as it was in ancient times.

The River Ganges, holy to Hindus, is the scene for many cremations.

SYMBOLISM

Rivers are so important to human life that they feature in many religions around the world. They often symbolise a barrier that divides life from death, or else their flow represents the eternal flow of life.

Below **The Indus River, which flows from its source in Tibet to the Arabian Sea.**

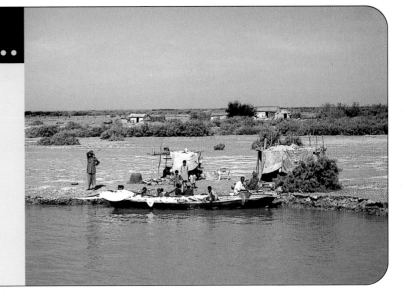

RIVERS AND TECHNOLOGY

Rivers have been used since ancient times for transport and as a source of power. Over the centuries developing technology has found ways to improve rivers for transport, and harness them as a source of power for industry.

CANALIZING RIVERS

A river that boats can travel along is said to be navigable. Many rivers have been changed to make them more navigable for large cargo ships. For instance, the River Rhine in Germany has been dredged to make it deeper and it is now navigable for over 800 km. Meanders on the Mississippi River in the USA have been straightened to let larger boats pass. After these changes, a river is said to be canalized, that is, more like a canal, although the water is still flowing.

Boats cannot travel where a river drops too steeply, but one answer is to build a lock and **weir**. A weir is a small step built across the river, and a lock is a small, enclosed section of the river in which the water level can be raised or lowered to allow boats to reach the water level above or below the weir.

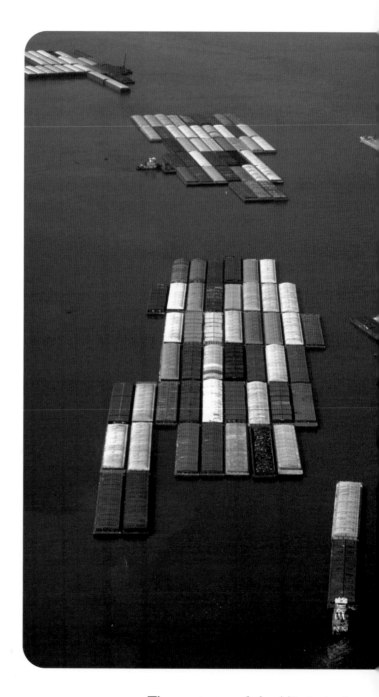

The vastness of the Mississippi River is seen here, where dozens of barges are herded together and transported downriver.

FACT FILE

CHINA'S WATERWAYS
- In 1949, China's new Communist government set about building a national network of waterways. Now China has over 100,000 km of navigable waterways.
- The Grand Canal, running 1,760 km from Beijing to Hangzhou, is the longest canal in the world. It was begun over 2,400 years ago.
- On the mountainous Yangtze and Wu Rivers, strong steel cables pull boats safely over dangerous rapids.

BENOIT FOURNEYRON

In 1827 a young Frenchman, Benoit Fourneyron, invented the water **turbine**, a much smaller and more efficient version of the traditional huge waterwheel. During Fourneyron's lifetime scientists scoffed at his invention, but his work was far ahead of its time. In 1895, 30 years after Fourneyron died, turbines were installed at the Niagara Falls to turn generators to produce electricity. Turbines are still widely in use today.

WATER POWER

River power has been in use since Roman times, when mills built beside rivers had large wooden waterwheels that turned a grindstone to grind grain or perform other tasks. In the nineteenth century, during the Industrial Revolution, factories sprang up wherever there was enough water to turn waterwheels. Waterwheels powered factory machinery, such as looms. In the twentieth century, new technology has been developed to harness water power to create electricity. This is called **hydroelectricity** (see pages 34–35).

This waterwheel was built in the nineteenth century to power a sawmill in Sherbrooke, Nova Scotia, Canada. Sherbrooke village is now a living history museum.

CROSSING THE RIVER

A river forms a natural barrier. Crossing the river safely – above, through or even under the water – is a great challenge to human ingenuity. Through the ages, new technology, materials and designs have developed to solve the ancient problem of crossing rivers.

The simplest way of crossing a stream or small river is to wade through at a shallow point, called a ford. Villages grew up at these traditional crossing points. Place names such as Bedford or Stratford often reflect their origin.

Around the world the first bridges were built out of natural materials, including stone blocks, felled tree-trunks, or ropes woven out of reeds or creepers. The Romans were the first to develop arched bridges. The first metal bridge was built of iron in 1779, over the River Severn at Ironbridge in the UK.

Over the past 200 years, revolutionary bridge designs have developed as new materials have come into use, including steel and reinforced concrete – concrete reinforced with metal inside. Today most bridges are built out of concrete.

FACT FILE

BRIDGE FACTS
• The Runyang Bridge across the mouth of the Yangtze River in China is due for completion in 2005. It will be the longest river crossing in the world. Its longest span is 1,490 m, and its total length is 23 km.
• The Gateshead Millennium Bridge (below) over the River Tyne in North-east England, opened in 2001. It is known as the 'blinking eye' bridge because it tips up – looking like a blinking eyelid – to let ships pass underneath.
• There are no bridges at all across the River Amazon. It is too wide to bridge safely. When the Amazon floods, it can reach up to 48 km wide!

The Gateshead Millennium Bridge is seen here tipped up to allow ships to pass under it. The bridge provides a footpath and cycleway linking the cities of Gateshead and Newcastle upon Tyne.

The Jiangyin Bridge over the River Yangtze in China was completed in 1999. It is a suspension bridge with a longest span of 1,385 m, making it the world's second-longest cable-suspended river bridge, after the Humber Bridge in the UK.

TUNNELS AND FERRIES

Tunnelling under a river is another way to cross the water. The first tunnel under the River Thames in London, UK, was completed in 1843 (there are now several of course). In 1998, work began on two double-decker road tunnels totalling 17.7 km under the River Seine in Paris, France, preserving the natural beauty of the river valley.

Ferries are another way of crossing a river, and they range from simple rowing boats to double- or triple-decker ships carrying cars, lorries and cargo.

Some ferries are very simple, like this boat in Bangladesh crossing the Meghna River.

DAMS AND RESERVOIRS

Rivers provide drinking water, but because rivers' flow can change they are unreliable sources of water. Building a dam is a way of allowing valuable fresh water to be stored and used when it is needed. Over the last hundred years, dams have been developed to provide a renewable source of energy as well.

A dam is a wall across a river which stops the water from flowing onwards. Small dams can be built out of earth and rocks but modern giant dams are built out of concrete. The 300 m-high Nurek Dam on the River Vakhsh in Tajikistan is the highest in the world.

When a dam is built the water rises behind it to fill the river valley. It forms an artificial lake, called a reservoir. Water is then let out in a regular flow, through drains in the dam. This is safer and more reliable than the river's seasonal changes.

This diagram shows how a dam works.

LOCATION FILE

THREE GORGES DAM ON CHINA'S YANGTZE RIVER

The Three Gorges Dam will be the largest hydroelectric dam in the world – over 1 km across, with a reservoir stretching over 560 km upstream. In 1989, local people's protests forced the Chinese government to suspend its plans for the dam, but construction work began after all in 1994 and the dam is now nearing completion.

River water held back by the dam creates a reservoir

Dam wall

Channel lets water out

Water flows through turbines, which create electricity

Electricity is carried around the country

Water is fed back into the river

HYDROELECTRICITY

The power of water flowing out through a dam can be harnessed to create hydroelectricity. As the water flows it turns turbines in the dam's drains, which generate electricity. The Hoover Dam on the Colorado River in the USA was completed in 1936. It was one of the earliest hydroelectric dams. Its reservoir, Lake Mead, is one of the largest artificial lakes in the world.

Hydroelectric dams can be productive, but they are hugely expensive to construct. The electricity may be too costly for ordinary local people. The environmental impact on the area is enormous, as the rising water drowns villages and towns in the valley. Hundreds of thousands of people can lose their homes when a large dam is built. Protestors argue that these huge projects are too expensive in poor, developing countries – especially if many people will lose their homes as a result.

The Glen Canyon Dam in Utah, USA, which was completed in 1963. It altered the flow of the Colorado River and has changed the ecosystem in the area.

 FACT FILE

DAM DISASTERS
• Almost 5,000 years ago, a dam on the River Nile failed during its first flood season. It was not correctly designed.
• A flash flood in 1889 in Pennsylvania, USA, caused a dam to break. Two thousand people were killed in an hour.
• In 1963, a landslide fell into the Vaiont Dam reservoir in Italy, producing a huge wave of water over the dam and killing 3,000 people. The dam was not seriously damaged.

ESTUARY ENERGY

Some river estuaries offer a source of renewable energy: tidal energy. In the estuary the river water mixes with the sea, flowing back and forth with the tides. The tide level rises and falls twice a day and this tidal change can be harnessed to generate electricity.

TIDE MILLS

Tidal energy has been used for centuries. From the eleventh century onwards, tide mills were built on river estuaries in the UK and along the Atlantic coasts of France and Spain. Most mills were used for grinding grain, and at Woodbridge on the River Deben in East Anglia, in the UK, the ancient tide mill is still working today. Centuries later, tide mills were built on river estuaries along the Atlantic coast in the USA and in Guyana, South America. They were used to crush sugar cane to produce sugar.

A traditional tidal mill on the River Rance in France at low tide.

FACT FILE

RENEWABLE ENERGY
• In 2001, renewable energy made up only 6 per cent of the USA's energy consumption.
• Renewable energy such as tidal energy is up to four times more costly than traditional fossil fuels such as coal or gas. But costs are falling as the technology develops.
• Governments around the world support the development of renewable energy. Wind energy is currently the fastest-developing source of renewable energy.

River estuaries such as this one in Nova Scotia, Canada, with a big difference between low and high tide, are the best sites for tidal power stations.

TIDAL ENERGY

In modern times, tidal power stations have been built or planned on river estuaries around the world. The best places are where there is a big difference between high and low tide. At the Bay of Fundy in Canada, the difference can be up to 20 m, the greatest in the world. Here, rapids are caused on the St John River by tidal water surging back up-river from the bay. Tidal energy was first considered in the Bay of Fundy in the 1920s, but has always been found to be too expensive and damaging to wildlife.

The Cardiff Bay Barrage in Wales has created a huge freshwater lake on the estuaries of the rivers Taff and Ely. Planners are exploring its potential for creating tidal energy. However, estuary mudflats offer important feeding and breeding grounds for many wading birds and other wildlife. Critics say that building estuary tidal power stations will harm a precious wildlife environment. So far, only a handful of tidal power stations have been constructed, the first being at La Rance in France.

LOCATION FILE

LA RANCE ESTUARY POWER STATION

The tidal power station at La Rance, France (right), opened in 1966. Across the 750 m-wide estuary of the River Rance is a barrage, or barrier. Tidal water can flow through the barrage in either direction. As the water flows, it turns generators which make electricity. The power station produces energy for around a million households.

La Rance estuary power station.

RIVERS IN FLOOD

When a river floods, water rises up and washes over its banks. The water can spread very quickly over flat land on either side. Some river floods, such as on the Nile, are regular and usually safe. Other floods are great disasters, causing huge damage and loss of life.

Rivers can flood for a number of reasons. Most floods happen when there is very heavy rainfall or rapid melting of snow. If the ground is already very wet and cannot take in any more water the rain runs quickly into rivers, which rise and cause flooding. Floods can also be caused by high tides sweeping up-river from the sea.

Flood disasters are one of the most costly type of natural disaster, sometimes killing hundreds or thousands of people. Rushing water brings torrents of mud and debris, and causes massive damage to homes, industry and agriculture. Vital services such as roads, railways and sewage systems can be swept away. When the Mississippi flooded in 1993, 30,000 homes were damaged. Repairs cost at least US$10 billion (£6.35 billion). The Yellow River has earned the nickname 'China's Sorrow'. It has caused some of the worst natural disasters of all time.

LOCATION FILE

THE RIVER ARNO, FLORENCE

The city of Florence, in north-west Italy, is famous for its historic art and architecture. In November 1966, the River Arno flooded to its highest level for 600 years. More than 1,000 paintings, 300,000 rare books and 700,000 historic documents were soaked or covered in black, smelly slime. Repair work went on for many years afterwards.

People using an improvised raft in a flooded street of Florence, during the flood of 1966.

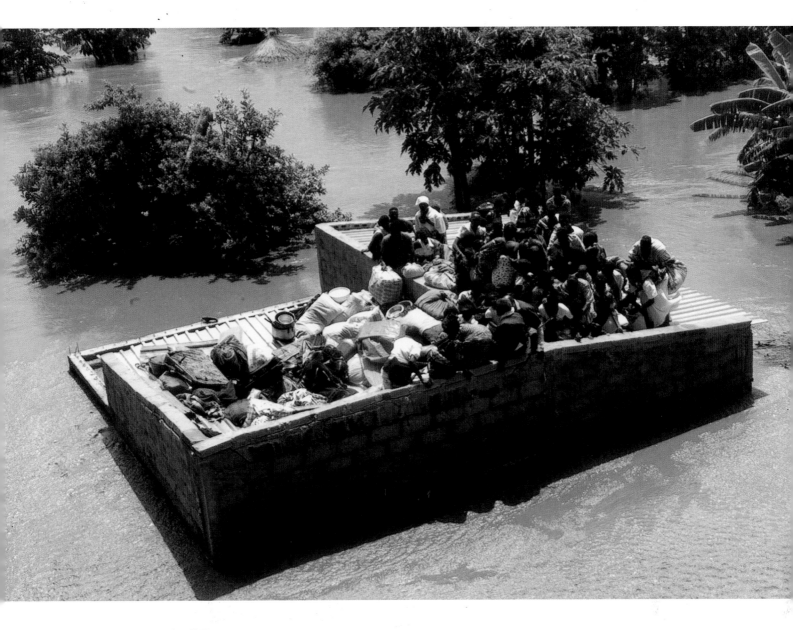

People in Mozambican floods in February 2000 wait on a rooftop to be rescued.

HUMAN INFLUENCE

In many parts of the world floods are growing more serious because of human influence. As well as cutting down forests, we are building more homes, roads and paved areas, as the world's population grows. These buildings make it harder for water to be absorbed into the ground. In cities, networks of drains carry the water quickly into the rivers. As a result, cities send more water at greater speed into the rivers than is natural. Building is also taking place on natural floodplains, with a high risk of flooding. All these factors make flooding more likely to happen – and more dangerous when it does.

 FACT FILE

RIVER FLOOD DISASTERS

The four greatest river flood disasters in recorded history have all been on two rivers in China:

LOCATION	DATE	ESTIMATED NUMBER KILLED
Yellow River	1931	3,700,000
Yellow River	1887	1,500,000
Yangtze River	1931	140,000
Yangtze River	1911	100,000

FLOOD DEFENCES

Floods are very dangerous, but building flood defences helps to reduce the risk. Some types of flood defences are very expensive, but there are many cheaper ways to help people to live safely near rivers.

LEVEES

One defence from flooding is to build a wall on top of the natural banks of the river, called a levee (say LEV-ay). Levees contain the river at a higher level without the water spilling over the top and flooding. Levees are built of concrete or, more cheaply, of earth and rock. At times of flood alert the levee can be made higher still with sandbags, rocks and soil. There is a danger, though, that the extra water is carried further downstream to flood elsewhere.

Above **Levees along the River Garonne in France protect Toulouse from the river breaking its banks and flooding the city.**

 LOCATION FILE

THE THAMES BARRIER

The River Thames flows through London, and for years people worried how to protect London from flooding caused by high tides and stormy winds. A large flood barrier (below) was completed in 1982. It has ten separate gates that can be closed when there is danger of a flood. This high-tech type of flood defence is effective, but expensive to construct.

The Thames Barrier in London, UK.

DREDGING

Another method of reducing the risk of flooding is to clear or dredge riverbeds to remove sediment and rocks that have gathered there, clogging it up. Clearing allows the river to hold more water.

PLANTING

Another solution is to plant trees on land near rivers. Trees remove water from the ground and release it into the air, which reduces the amount of water running down hillsides into streams and rivers. The tree roots also help to bind the earth together, reducing soil erosion – which in turn reduces the amount of sediment clogging up rivers.

SAFER BUILDING

In some heavily populated areas where land is in short supply, homes are built on low-lying land which is more at risk of flooding. Building homes on higher ground is a safer policy.

Dredging a harbour in Germany. Dredging makes the riverbed deeper so that large ships can use the river.

 FACT FILE

ANCIENT AND MODERN FLOOD DEFENCES

• In ancient Egypt, 960 km of levees were built along the west bank of the River Nile from Aswan to the Mediterranean.

• Levees were first built on the banks of the Mississippi River in the USA in the early eighteenth century.

• Over 5,600 km of raised levees have been built along the Mississippi and its tributaries, but some are now being removed, as they are costly to maintain, and they simply shift the problem of flooding downstream. Instead, certain areas are set aside to take floodwater where it can do no harm.

LEISURE AND TOURISM

Rivers are great places to relax and have fun. Rivers attract anglers, walkers and campers who enjoy the natural surroundings. New river sports such as whitewater rafting are growing in popularity. Leisure use of rivers is increasing as tourism grows around the world, but tourism brings its own dangers to wildlife and the environment.

FISHING

Angling, or fishing, is an ancient sport. A 2,400-year-old Chinese account tells of fishing with a silk line, using cooked rice as bait. In many countries today, more people take part in angling than in any other sport. As angling is restricted in many rivers to protect fish stocks, fishing in artificial lakes stocked with freshwater fish has become popular.

Some campaigners argue that fishing is a cruel sport that harms fish and other wildlife. Fishing lines, lead weights and nets can harm birds and fish if they are left in the water. Anglers argue that they help to look after the environment and protect fish.

LOCATION FILE

RIVER SJOA, NORWAY

Norway's River Sjoa is a popular destination for whitewater rafting and many other outdoor sports. From a base at Randsverk, high in the mountains, holidaymakers can try out potholing, fishing and mountaineering as well as whitewater rafting.

An American whitewater rafting team battles with the waters of the Zambesi River in Africa.

NEW RIVER SPORTS

Canoeing, or kayaking, as it is also known, became a popular sport in the nineteenth century. Canoeing became an Olympic event for the first time in 1924. In 1972, canoe slalom or whitewater canoeing was introduced as a new Olympic event, where canoes had to navigate through gates, rapids and falls in a river. New river sports are developing all the time, including hydro glisse (from the French, meaning 'water sliding'), which involves riding down a river holding on to a special board.

Travel companies offer whitewater rafting activity holidays in wild and beautiful surroundings, on rivers such as the Zambezi in Africa. Tourism brings many benefits to local traders, but it can also threaten fragile ecosystems. Too many tourists visiting a region damage the very environment that attracted them in the first place.

Families enjoy a beach on the River Rhine in Germany. The Rhine was extensively cleaned up in the 1970s–1990s, having become badly polluted.

FACT FILE

RIVER TOURISM AROUND THE WORLD

- Turkey's government is developing river sports tourism on the River Göksu, while protecting its important bird wildlife.
- In 2002, Cambodia, Laos and Vietnam spent US$35 million (£22 million) to attract tourists to the Mekong River in Asia. Piers, walking trails and information centres were built along the river.
- Botswana, in southern Africa, has developed a National Eco-Tourism Strategy for the Chobe River to develop tourism and conserve the environment.

RIVERS FOR LIFE

Fresh water from rivers is a vital resource for life. Modern daily life, especially in developed countries in the West, demands more and more fresh water for industry, agriculture and homes. We must protect and share the Earth's river water fairly to preserve life and the environment for the future.

USING WATER

In the West, each person uses twenty times more water than in the poorest countries. New methods of agriculture need extra irrigation, for example growing luxury crops such as flowers in hot climates. This means more and more water is diverted from rivers, especially in countries where rainfall is very low and crops need more irrigation.

A bridge over the Yellow River in China, where it ran dry in 1997.

The amount of water drawn from a river needs to be controlled and managed, because if too much water is taken out of a river it can dwindle or run dry. People living downstream may not have enough water, and the remaining water may become heavily polluted. Many rivers around the world are running dry. China's Yellow River ran dry in its lower reaches for seven months in 1997. This deprived Shadong Province of its water for irrigation. Shadong produces one-fifth of China's maize and one-seventh of its wheat.

RIVERS IN TROUBLE

• The level of the inland Aral Sea in Asia has dropped by over 16 m in the past 50 years. This is because so much water is taken out of its two main source rivers.

• Over 90% of the natural flow of the River Nile is used for irrigation or is lost through evaporation, especially from reservoirs.

• One in four people in the world does not have clean drinking water, and has no choice but to drink from polluted rivers or wells.

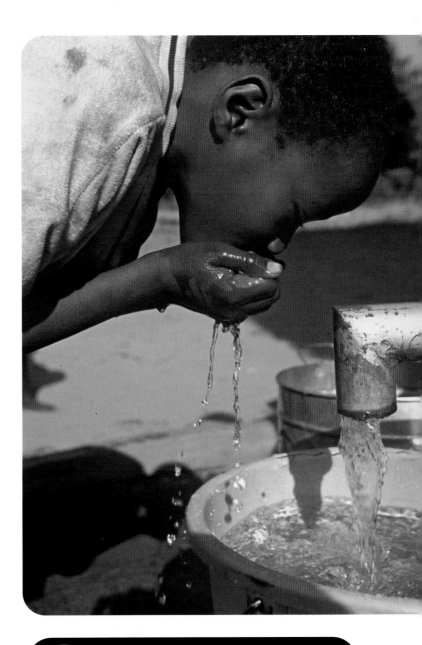

A child drinks from a tap bringing clean water, installed by the charity WaterAid. WaterAid is dedicated to providing safe water, sanitation and hygiene education to the world's poorest people.

WATER IN WAR – AND PEACE

Water is such a precious resource for life that it can be a target during war. During many wars in the twentieth century, dams have been bombed to destroy the water supply for industry and to cause flooding. In 1999 Serbian forces contaminated water supplies during the war in Kosovo.

Water wars may arise in the future where there are rival claims to water. To avoid this danger, many countries are working together to share and protect river water flowing through their lands. For instance the River Zambezi crosses or forms the boundaries of six countries in Southern Africa. International agreements between some of these countries have helped to share the water more fairly, to protect those downstream.

MEKONG RIVER, ASIA

Four of the countries along the Mekong River – Cambodia, Laos, Thailand, Vietnam – signed an agreement in 1995 to safeguard the river. They agreed to protect the water and the river environment, to protect shipping rights, and to make joint decisions about how much water to take out of the river.

GLOSSARY

Canal A narrow, man-made waterway, made for irrigation or for boats to travel along.

Canyon A deep gorge or ravine.

Condense Turn from a vapour into a liquid, for example turn from steam into water.

Dam A wall built across a river or stream to hold back water.

Delta A place where a river flows in many channels out into the sea.

Discharge The amount of water flowing in a river.

Drainage area The area of land that drains into a river.

Dredge To scoop soil and sediment from the bottom of a river to deepen or clear it.

Erode To wear away rocks and soil by water, wind or ice.

Estuary The wide, tidal part of a river, where it leads into the sea.

Exploit To make use of, to make gain out of.

Flash flood A sudden, severe flood caused by heavy rain.

Glacier A huge frozen river of slow-moving ice.

Groundwater Fresh water that is underground, contained within the rocks and soil.

Hydroelectricity Electricity that is generated when flowing water turns a turbine, usually in a dam.

Irrigation Supplying crop plants with water via channels or pipes in order to help them to grow.

Meander The loops and curves made by a slow-moving river.

Mudflats The muddy area revealed at the mouth of a river when the tide is out.

Porous Having little holes, which allow water to pass through.

Rapids A steep section of a river where the water flows fast over rocks.

Renewable energy Energy created from sources such as water, wind and sun, that are not used up by creating the energy.

Reservoir An artificial lake for storing water.

Saturated Holding as much water or liquid as it is able to.

Sediment Little bits of rocks and soil that are carried by a river.

Source The origin or head of a river.

Spring A source, an outflow of water from a rock.

Tributaries A stream that runs into another.

Turbine A rotary motor, with a wheel or drum with curved fins, that is driven by water or steam to generate electricity.

Wadi The bed of an ancient river through a desert, that is usually dry.

Water cycle The circulation of the Earth's water, in which it evaporates from the sea, lakes and rivers to the air, and turns back to a liquid to fall as rain or snow.

Weir A dam across a river.

FURTHER INFORMATION

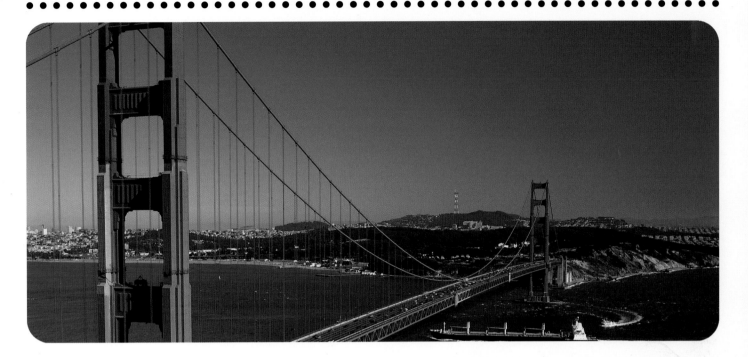

Above **The Golden Gate Bridge links San Francisco and the Marin Peninsula in California, USA. It was completed in 1937.**

WEBSITES TO VISIT

www.irn.org
News about International Rivers Network's efforts to support local communities working to protect their rivers.
International Rivers Network
1847 Berkeley Way
Berkeley, CA 94703, USA
Tel: +1 510 848 1155
Email: info@irn.org

www.wateraid.org.uk
WaterAid is an international non-governmental organization dedicated to providing safe water, sanitation and hygiene education to the world's poorest people.
WaterAid
Prince Consort House, 27–29 Albert Embankment
London SE1 7UB, UK
Tel: 020 7793 4500
Email: wateraid@wateraid.org

www.wrc.wa.gov.au/protect/waterways/index.htm
The website of Waterways WA, Western Australia's waterways management programme, about protecting rivers, creeks, wetlands and estuaries.
Waterways and Rivers Commission
Level 2, Hyatt Centre, 3 Plain Street
East Perth 6004, Western Australia
Tel: +61 08 9278 0300
Email: waterways.wa@wrc.wa.gov.au

BOOKS TO READ

Themes in Geography: *Rivers* by Fred Martin (Heinemann Library, 1996)

Earth Alert!: *Rivers* by Shelagh Whiting (Hodder Wayland and WWF UK, 2001)

Mapping Earthforms: *Rivers* by Catherine Chambers (Heinemann Library, 2001)

A River Journey: *The Amazon* by Simon Scoones, ***The Ganges*** by Rob Bowden, ***The Mississippi*** by Martin Curtis, ***The Nile*** by Rob Bowden, ***The Rhine*** by Ronan Folay and ***The Yangtze*** by Rob Bowden (Hodder Wayland, 2003)

Earthfiles: *Rivers and Lakes* by Chris Oxlade (Heinemann Library, 2003)

Nature on the Rampage: *Floods* by Tami Deedrick (Raintree, 2004)

INDEX